Leaving Camustianavaig

Leaving CAMUSTIANAVAIG

POEMS BY
John Beaton

WORD GALAXY PRESS
An imprint of Able Muse Press

Word Galaxy Press

www.wordgalaxy.com

Printed in the United States of America

Library of Congress Cataloging-in-Publication Data

Names: Beaton, John, 1952- author.
Title: Leaving Camustianavaig / poems by John Beaton.
Description: San Jose, CA : World Galaxy Press, an imprint of Able Muse Press, 2020.
Identifiers: LCCN 2019059838 (print) | LCCN 2019059839 (ebook) | ISBN 9781773490625 (paperback) | ISBN 9781773490632 (digital)
Subjects: LCGFT: Poetry.
Classification: LCC PR9199.4.B4337 L43 2020 (print) | LCC PR9199.4.B4337 (ebook) | DDC 811/.6--dc23
LC record available at https://lccn.loc.gov/2019059838
LC ebook record available at https://lccn.loc.gov/2019059839

Cover image: *Talisker Bay, Skye* by Joshua Earle

Cover & book design by Alexander Pepple

Word Galaxy Press is an imprint of Able Muse Press—at www.ablemusepress.com

Word Galaxy Press
467 Saratoga Avenue #602
San Jose, CA 95129

Contents

Leaving Camustianavaig

Headwaters

Wilderness

Forests

Sounds

The River

Women of the Valley

Echoes

The Sea

Reflections

Leaving Camustianavaig

Headwaters

Stillbirth

I

The day I left for Canada my mother
and father quelled their tears. We held and hugged.
He said, "We three may never see each other
      alive again." That leaving
      hooked my gut and tugged.

We never did. He died and left her widowed
so next time we three met was at his tomb.
Our parting afterwards had been foreshadowed—
      the breakage of the cord
      that fed me from her womb.

We rode on gondolas to summits she
had never dreamed of. Mountains could not buy
her heart from where they'd raised the family—
      we shared reunions linked
      by contrails in the sky.

II

Hi, Mum. It's me, from Canada, your John.
Och, John! You've caught me in an awful state!
I know. I'm sad to hear that Henry's gone.
      The one that was my brother?
      My memory's not great.

He's back now, from the War. Oh dear, they're here.
Who? *They're all against me.* Who? *The clique.*
They've done such nasty things. They say I'm queer.
    I think I'll kill myself.
    So how's the house this week?

Och this one's grand. I moved two days ago.
And Johnny helped. I think he's at the door.
I'll have to run now, Henry. Cheerio.
    Don't go. The phone is dead.
    The cord exists no more.

III

A winter storm comes swooping down the hills
and, gusting, blasts umbrellas inside-out.
They ring the grave like blighted daffodils
    and rain-black mourners hold,
    like buffeted peat-burn trout.

I take the tasselled pall rope, let it slide,
and with my brothers ease the coffin down;
it slips across the lip of a great divide
    and sinks what was my mother—
    a shuck, a wrinkled gown.

Gales carry off the prayer as it is spoken.
I cast the rope adrift. The rains of Skye
slap my back. Again, a cord has broken—
    this time my lungs won't fill.
    I try but cannot cry.

Laying Ghosts to Rest

My father, raised in Skye, believed in ghosts.
I went with him to feed the hens at night
and came to share his fear that hellish hosts
were prowling in the trees just out of sight.

At ten years old I thought it time to purge
this nonsense from my mind. One night I walked
two long, dark miles to where I planned to scourge
myself with wraiths by whom I might be stalked:

Kilmorack Churchyard. I unlatched the gate
and entered. Gravestones, indistinct and dim,
loomed round me and I felt the hand of Fate
come close, no doubt to tear me limb from limb.

My teacher told us once that Thomas Gray,
a poet, said the dead led gentle lives
as village folk who whiled their years away
as ordinary husbands, kids, and wives.

That thought came ghosting back; foreboding fled
and all I sensed was kinship, sadness, peace,
and freedom from suspicion that the dead
have bones to pick with those they predecease.

My father's in the darkness now, alone.
On writing this, the thought occurs to me
that maybe I should stand before his stone
and read him Thomas Gray's dear elegy.

Brothers of the Byre

The byre cleaves to the half-floor my father and uncle barrow-mixed
and trowelled. I imprinted my boy's hand in its wetness. Then, rock by rock,
they raised the walls from broken crag, built rafters where iron was fixed
and there they kept the scythe, bridle, and trammel under lock
that went unfastened. I stared at knotted beams in days when rain
beelined down corrugated iron and dropped like handlines through fingers,
through tar smells, through dung steam rising to mist the lowering sky's dank
    pane;
then weather came. Wind sledged below the roof—my memory lingers
on the wedge and the rend of the gusts; up-arched, the sheeting lever-ripped
and flapped. Persuading nails, the brothers crawled like earwigs under
a King's Gold sky, shining in the black of their oilskins. As last rains dripped,
they hung their work with rope and rocks. Villagers followed the thunder;
the years that rolled like Easter stones left caves, not resurrections,
and nets hung dry; rust stalked the waves of the eaves. One year or other
they buried her miscarried baby where the byre now stands—old recollections
of crosswise sticks, of wildflower bunches were marks of my older brother,
my mother tells me now. We stare at it, hand holding hand;
I sense the beseeching fingers reaching higher, ever higher,
to clasp the handprint that dimples the floor, to be raised to the stormy land
our father and uncle worked together—brothers of the byre.

Regeneration

Hay ripens. I sharpen my tapering scythe blade
and chamfer its wafer of paper-thin steel
with stone swoops; it's hooked like a peregrine's talon.
The snaking shaft sweeps and the first swathe is side-laid
beside me, clean slain. As I swing I can feel
the gravid field yielding. Sheaves kneel and then fall in
the breeze in formation. Their early seeds dance there
like next April's rain showers shining in air.
The cocksfoot and rye grass and fescue are falling,
the rogue oats, the sedges—I harvest the field where
they shaded the clover and none do I spare.
The sun sets on stubble where hay stalks lie sprawling.
My father stood here in the old days like one
of the stalks that made hay as they fell in the sun.

Legacy

Inside his penthouse office
he views his Inuit artwork,
carvings from a culture
reduced to buy-and-hold,
then scans the evening city,
his bar chart on the skyline
      where real estate has grown his stake
      but cost him bonds he's had to break—
      he hadn't meant to so forsake
his parents. They looked old

that day outside the croft house
when cowed farewells were murmured
as cattle lowed in wind blasts
keening from the sea.
His mother and his father
stood waving from the porch step;
      next year she'd crack her pelvic bone,
      when winter iced that slab of stone,
      and never walk again. *I'll phone*,
and he was history.

On history—the cailleach,
her mother, at the peat-fire,
would offer mint imperials
from a Coronation tin,
then draw her shawl around them
and spin him, in the Gaelic,

tales of what had gone before,
the penances his people bore.
    Now, as his mind replays that lore,
he pours another gin.

She'd tell him how *The old ones*
foreclosed the feudal factors
from forcing emigration
to "lands of endless loam."
One night she said *Some hopefuls*
believed it and they boarded.
    The day they sailed, a boy was found
    upon the shore. The soul had drowned—
    they said he'd leapt into the sound
and tried to swim back home.

Be glad your parents battled
the lords and laws for tenure
and stoned the bold militia
to get the Crofting Act.
That's why they can't evict us
as long as family members
    remain upon, and work, the land.
    Aye, many a generation's manned
    this croft. It's passed from hand to hand—
be sure it's kept intact.

Next day he walked a headland
and brooded on that body
swaying in wave-flung flotsam,

now neither here nor there;
then, standing like a Culdee
enrobed by gales, he gazed on
  the mists and hills and holms and voes
  the boy had loved so much he chose
  to swim the wake, in which he froze.
He wondered *Would I dare?*

Then, seeing an osprey stone-dive,
he knew he'd fall for fortune;
no wake for him—a contrail
was his umbilical cord.
He'd visited three years back
to mark his mother's passing
  and wishes now he'd stayed until
  he'd overcome his father's will—
  his glass is low, another fill—
he'd tried. How he'd implored.

The bodach had resisted:
I'm not a man for cities
and, son, you know I'll always
work this land for you
in case you change your thinking
or yet beget a crofter.
  Come by the fire and feel the heat—
  I cut and dried those blocks of peat.
  I grow and catch enough to eat,
there's nothing more to do.

He downs his drink and glances
again at his computer—
an email from a neighbour:
Your father died last night.
He'd lately gotten thinner
and seldom had a fire on—
    what little peat he had was soft.
    Some things of yours are in the loft
    so mind them when you sell the croft.
The city lights are bright;

he turns again and faces
his metamorphic sculptures
of walruses in soapstone
that never will break free
from rock that locks the sea waves—
past fused against the future.
    Another gin? That's six. Or eight?
    So be it. Clarity's too late.
    His real estate's no real estate—
he's left his legacy.

Leaving Camustianavaig

Portree Cemetery

Today we leave the croft and you
and, though the rain-mist makes it vague,
we see your chosen gravesite view
ploughing the clouds—Ben Tianavaig.

We see its bracken patches spring
by dykes you built, where bogs of peat
lie spaded out for winter heat,
how sheep paths terrace slopes of ling,

and how the freshet gravitates
to where, as tykes, you fished the burns
and played by byres and butter churns,
on Sundays ate from heirloom plates.

You left us that bespoken land
but cloud has claimed the graveyard's view—
the mighty plough is buried and
your offspring leave the croft to you.

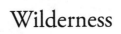

Wilderness

Wolves

I'm wakened, drawn towards the ice-thin window,
to witness scenes as faint and still as death.
How bleak the moon; how bare the trees and meadows;
    sky's pale maw overhangs
    Earth bleached beneath star fangs.
    Night's curled lip sneers on shadows
    of mountains set like teeth.

Two bow waves shear the median of the valley,
iced hayfield yields as feral muscles glide—
hoarfrost disturbed by wakes of live torpedoes.
    Grey shoulders breach and lope,
    implode and telescope,
    impelled by ruthless credos
    of chilled and vicious pride.

The wolves tear savage furrows down the nightscape;
their eyes are shined with blood, their mission clear.
Grass springs back shocked to green behind their passage—
    twin tracks traverse the vales,
    cold comets trailing tails
    leave scarred in frost their message:
    the wolves, the wolves passed here.

Baying at Two Moons

The moon is full above Mount Inglismaldie
and mirrored on obsidian Two Jack Lake;
the nights are growing long, but no Vivaldi
concertos leap the seasons' firebreak—

there's silence. Now a lone coyote flows
along the bank. Then, head raised like a seal
balancing a moon-ball on her nose,
poises to un-throat a call. I feel

her loneliness—she's come so close to me
it seems as though she may have lost a mate
and sensing me has sparked an urge to yowl
to any living thing for company,

but, even so, I don't anticipate
the utter woebegoneness of her howl.

Lost Overnight in the Woods

The horizon garrottes the twilight's throat. I sleepwalk
through slash and over deadfall. My arms, white canes,
antenna me through copses; touching tree trunks,
legs of huge tenebrios, whose abdomens
are canopies of darkness under elytra,
I walk. Winds whisper mantra after mantra.

Now branches frieze the sky—wrought iron frost-work
Sistines the darkling beetles' undersides.
I see an Agincourt arrow, a kingfisher, flash-track,
grey, but fletched with blurs of blues and reds,
through ribs of fallen trees that cage a reach
where swans' necks question whether day will break.

A bull elk rears. His forelegs scissor the moon-rays.
He splashes down, legs thrashing the water, then dips
his head in the glister, raises his rack like a sunrise,
shakes it, smithereening his crown, then grasps
the horizon's rope in his antlers; with a swing and a sling,
throws bolas at darkness's legs and unstrangles the sun.

Forests

Caledonian Pines

The pines stand tall upon the lochan isles;
the ancient Woods of Caledon, they're all
that's left untouched by centuries of fire,
man's pall—a shroud of smoke from bens to kyles.

Age-toughened, brittle, jagged, grey of limb,
half-fossilised, these hardy few survive,
remaindered by their moats of mountain rain,
alive, small stands, their yield not worth the swim.

Held high before their former fiefdom's hills,
last green crowns cock to high ground, heather-skinned;
old clans alone, their branches seed with moans
the wind that bears them barren freedom's chills.

Wildfire

It starts with lightning, tinder, and a gust.
Smoke-jumper teams, at this stage, may contain it—
clad in Nomex, 'chuting down to dust
they rip along the fire line like a bayonet,
swinging pulaskis, cleaving to clearings and creeks,
drip-torching back fires, containing each hot spot
with counter-tides of flame. They know physiques
honed to sprint with gear may still be caught
by racing fronts and panic, so they pack
an aluminium drape, a fire shelter.
A flare-up—now they cannot reach the black
by racing through the flame wall, helter-skelter,
so they deploy before the terra torch
and bake like foiled potatoes in its scorch.

The fire expands. Its roaring conflagration
finds ladder fuels and candles standing trees.
The incident commander starts to station
resources round the burn's peripheries—
machinery and hotshot crews assemble
in camps and helibases. Like mirages,
infernos rise to ridgelines, flare, and tremble.
As faller teams and swampers check barrages
of lowland flame, a bucket-swinging Bell
lathers long control lines with retardant.
The Super Huey heli-crews rappel;
Sikorsky sky-cranes suck and buzz like ardent
mosquitoes, but combustion's alchemies
still plate the skies with gold. A rising breeze....

The crowning flames become a firestorm
as fires' heads combine. Convection columns
shoot limbs and embers upwards where they form
flak for tanker crews. Smoke overwhelms
visibility. They drop a Mars
and lift great lumps of lake, on every mission
seven thousand gallons salving scars
from summer's branding iron. Sudden fission
caused by sap expanding inside trunks
sends frissons of crackling sparks across the blaze
as firecracker trees explode. The thunks
of falling tops spook ground crews. Flames find ways
to lope the overstorey under cover
of smoke while dozers doze and choppers hover.

Although we fight it, such spontaneous heat
kindles inner duff. Like Icarus
we're drawn to flame as if it could complete
combustion of some smouldering in us,
a splendour in the trees. With rolls and dips,
like waxwings, flying wax wings to the sun,
we soar. . . . And then, as if a flash eclipse
confronts us with the dark side of the moon,
the aftermath appears: black devastation,
burnt poles, which yesterday were foliaged.
Cracked pods already seed reforestation
and years will heal what fire so quickly aged
but now, devoid of even twigs and slash,
this moonscape marks where sunlight fell as ash.

The Combustion of Apples

Old Gravenstein, your boughs are scabbed and mossy
but you expand them graciously, a host
inviting passers-by to share the glossy
hospitality your bushels boast.

Your blossom spangled spring rain's spectrumed prism
and dropped; green stippled you and turned to reds
and golds. They coalesce—spring's pointillism
is smeared as autumn's flaring wildfire spreads.

Now fanning winds gust leaves—sparks float to earth
and apples fall like coals. They'll leave a tortured
candelabrum etched above a hearth
where ash still smokes—the frosted misty orchard.

Dusk. Across the mural of the sky
your portraitist depicts another scene:
he specks and flecks your boughs with nebulae
in blooms of carmine, salmon, gilt, and green.

And they too blend as space dust avalanches
down columns light years tall and then combines
in worlds that fall, like apples from your branches,
decaying as their core-stored sun declines.

Thus apple trees and galaxies expire:
in dappled glades of universal fire.

Sounds

Year-Leap

This field in winter forms a wetland, quiet
except for hushing rainfall, rushing hail,
a breeze that, fussed with snowflakes, seems to sigh at
the calls of robin, chickadee, and quail,
and swishing noises as a buck picks through
a copse of wild roses, red with thorns,
briar stems, and rose hips, which he'll chew
as velvet slowly silences his horns.

And then the frogs! These mudlark choristers,
raucous for amplexus, now rejoice—
last night we heard no chirrups, chirps, or chirrs;
tonight they'd overwhelm a stentor's voice—
and, swamping winter with their song, they bring
good news: the year is sound, and crouched to spring.

Murmuration

There is a blackness like a furl of smoke
hurtling and twisting fast across the sky—
     it shudders and explodes
     and shards of shrapnel fly
upwards, bursting, bursting, then condense,
cascading down, and cresting to bespatter
the air above us as the starlings scatter,
     and then the flock implodes,
flattens once again, and forms a cloak
of undulating wingbeats, recompense
     for having had the sense
to go outside and see the things that matter.

Songs of the Isles

It's Celtic Chaos at Loch Duich. The music session's finishing.
The barman pours folks out the door. They drive away diminishing—
vanishing into darkening glens, where Clearances once shattered
the homes and lives of crofting peoples; the sheep now flourish, scattered
like grace notes fallen from fiddle airs, or from songs of bygone aeons—
of Flodden's and Culloden's fields, and spray-sodden Hebrideans.
All night they stamped their musical feet and swirled the smoke and ale,
with claps and birls and hoochs and skirls, now silent, still, and stale.

And I return to Plockton's shore, where I sit on a stone and wonder
whether I would've made a man among men, in the days of plight and plunder,
in the days when allegiances could shift, like seafarers under sail
changing course to avail themselves of the winds that would prevail.
This very dawn I stood upon the buttress across the bay,
the watch-crag of Loch Carron's narrows, where lookouts perhaps one day
sentried these Viking longship routes from Ivar Blacktooth's pillagers
as his ravaging band swung inland to ravish the wives of villagers.

Before me lie the sheltered coves where the sailboats raced today.
Now their wooden hulls heave sideways, as the tide-wash ebbs away,
but their lapstrake lines and their gleaming curves seem to come alive again
and take to the waves of the Inner Sound like a timeless song's refrain.
And I see two square sails billowing as they swallow long sea miles—
the dragon ship of Somerled, Lord of all these Isles,
passes Eilann Donan's fort propelled by forty-eight oarsmen
flexing brawn to the beat of a gong to ram the fleeing Norsemen.

And Cathula beats that gong in tune to muscle and sweat and wave—
her tawny hair howls in the dark; she's his mistress and his brave
second mate in battles and surprise nighttime attacks
that set the coarse invaders to their oars with flailing backs.
With two hundred Irish gallowglasses, and with smoke and sleight of hand,
he routed a thousand Vikings; and with the will to understand
the needs of men who rally to the stronger shield and blade
he won his frays in minds, not bays, by allegiances he made.

I see beached goblet sterns becalmed, like the locals' sleeping faces.
Our hearts in song's communion rose; I saw the shimmering traces
of unfulfilled but fervent longing, in glances, bare and vulpine,
watching sea lochs simmering red, dark as quaichs of mulled wine.
And I realize that just like them, I'm another whose dreams of glory
are doomed to nullity for they come too late in history's story;
that I can love their songs and tunes, but I'll never swear an oath
or wager countless lives upon a windblown clansman's troth,

or snap my neck from the axe's path, or swing my sword in wrath,
or walk among the dead and maimed in the battle's aftermath,
or choose my friends for their usefulness, for repute of non-betrayal,
or commit my hand to venturings where death awaits all who fail.
And so I rise from my foreshore stone with a drowsiness in my head
and cross the road and climb the stairs and go to my safe warm bed,
while the mute musicians lie in theirs in their glens of bleating song
and dream of fiddles, the wind-filled flute, the bodhran, and the gong.

Music Maker

With joy, this handmade violin
I give to you. Through thick and thin
we've held each other, skin to skin,
     in adoration,
knowing together we would win,
     and share, elation.

Enjoy. You gave me such elation
that I commissioned this violin—
a token of what it meant to win
     your love; a thin
label inscribes the adoration
     inked under my skin.

The spruce wood draws a flawless skin
across its back, reflects elation
to the high air. In adoration
     this violin
will serenade, when light grows thin,
     the night to win.

But when in time we cannot win,
when varnish cracks upon our skin
and hair upon our bow grows thin,
     that raw elation,
revived, will sing from this violin—
     our adoration.

We'll always have this adoration
for one another. I would win
you, life lived over. Violin
        notes silk my skin,
scrolling out the bow's elation,
        unction thin.

The finest times of life are thin
moments when waves of adoration
sweep us on to seek elation—
        to vie and win
the thrill that dances down our skin
        to a violin.

This air is thin. You sigh—I win
the gift of adoration. Our skin
strokes elation's violin.

Your Voice

Some pages have no signatures
yet I don't doubt which writing's yours—
it bears a voice print so, with ease,
I know you finger-stroked the keys
or made the helpless ballpoint jink
along your curves and drool its ink.
But living voice has pace and tone,
and tongue—I feel an urge to phone
when you're away to hear that purr
across your vocal cords, that burr
of huskiness as lips sough vowels
from registers where ardour growls,
to hear your tongue-tip palate-dance
and castanet your consonants
as, from boleros in your mind,
your thoughts, in whirls of words, unwind.

Your voice is no mere human flute;
its concert organ finds the root
position in your innate score
and plays your music, lets it soar
through the cathedral of your chest
where, underneath your lifting breast,
your heartbeat's muted tremolo
vibrates through breathing's cello bow,
the whole ensemble playing Bach
and Bruckner, Brahms, and Bacharach
to universes, yet à deux.
You speak and blind men fall for you.

Midwinter Music

Orkney

The hawthorn branches' lightning lines
are paralleled by seams of white
as snowfall mantles them, each jagged
    angle traced,
      each pronged and ragged
fork embalmed, perhaps embraced.

Around the fields, old stunted pines
grow flocculent with flakes. Despite
the fires within, the farms are wooled
    with snow, their sills
      and gutters ruled
and cushioned with small corniced hills.

The drystone dykes have scalloped crests.
On open moors, the windwards sides
of standing stones blockade the blow,
    black and upright,
      till driving snow
feathers them into background white.

The moaning wind stravaigs and quests
but one communal call abides—
as flurries hover, glide, and fall
    among the drifts,
      inside a hall
a cellist's hand position-shifts.

The River

Shadow-casting

Cast your line towards the sun;
let your shadow fall behind you.
Face the glare, absorb its stun,
and cast your line towards the sun
for casting shade makes wild things run;
so face the brightness though it blind you—
cast your line towards the sun
and let your darkness fall behind you.

And a River Runs through Me

I come to gaps in the path by the Ferry Pool,
spaces lost to spates that banked and bored
its bend while I was gone. My mind is full
of remembered days when I once sat and pored
over my books in my father's country school,
dreaming of greenheart rods we couldn't afford,

and of finnock and sea trout shoaling in Hercher's Ford
as the flow tide shouldered into this Ferry Pool.
I tried to concentrate, but the only school
that didn't leave me disengaged and bored
was the one that glittered where the tide-wash poured,
waiting to charge upstream when the moon was full.

It's not that I was an underprivileged fool.
We had a respectable car. My father's Ford
Prefect performed if sufficient oil was poured
into its smoky innards. It managed to pull
up Drumnadrochit Hill with us all aboard
from summer holidays, coming back to school.

But the Beauly River was my personal school—
the lore in its libraries was plentiful
and in its study, I went overboard,
seeking the deepest passages I could ford,
deciphering the runes of every pool,
as down its glen the ancient waters poured,

histories over which I daily pored,
even when meant to be listening at school.
Casting a Teal, Blue, and Silver, I'd feel a pull,
then hear my name too late and, like a fool,
not be able to answer. I could afford
distraction then. But later I couldn't look bored

while doing my city job in front of a board,
couldn't contemplate the flows that since have poured
down from this Ferry Pool to Hercher's Ford
where still, by standing waves, the sea trout school
and haunt the eddies when the tide grows full.
Many's the dusk at the tail glide of this pool,

worlds away from the boardroom and the school,
when moonlight poured and the curve of the path was full,
I cast to the lip of the ford. I feel the pull.

Jock Scott

He screws the collet vice to pinch a down-eyed limerick hook
and winds the Pearsall's silk around itself—his scissors clip it—
then lays abutting turns along the shank to near the crook,
and there he ties in black-barred strands of golden pheasant tippet.

And now some crimson Indian crow, a butt of ostrich herl
entrapping silver tinsel and a length of yellow floss;
the body's bottom half evolves as floss revolves; each twirl
of ribbing, like an elver, spirals upwards and across.

"Jim, stop. We're out of kindling and the dogs have gotten free;
another slate is off the roof; the kitchen ceiling's leaking.
You'll have to go to work soon and you haven't made my tea.
Next time you say I'm lazy, just you look at who is speaking."

"I'll do those jobs this minute, Jean. I rose before day dawned
and tying flies won't interfere with chores I have to tackle."
That night he ties the middle butt, a tutu of toucan frond,
then lays the second body half—black floss, wide rib, black hackle.

He ties the second hackle in, guinea fowl on the quill,
then trims it with a razor blade and strokes the thread with wax;
two slips of white-tipped turkey tail come next to under-fill
the over-wings he'll build and tie in mirrored upright stacks.

Yellow, scarlet, blue—he cuts dyed filaments of swan,
and interlocks their fibre hairs with golden pheasant tail,
some peacock sword-herl, speckled bustard, bustard florican,
married with teal, barred summer duck, beneath brown mallard's veil.

42

He ties in two blue chatterer cheeks and gives their stubs a cropping;
from his most precious cape he adds bold eyes of jungle cock.
Inside a glass he'd set a wetted golden pheasant topping—
it crests the Jock Scott's silhouette, a curving air-dried lock.

The tapered head, and varnish. "Come, MacKenzie, shake a leg.
What fly should I be using for this time of year and water?"
"Your big Jock Scott without a doubt. It's like a powder keg
exploding down among the fish. Milord, you'll make a slaughter."

Three fish—the fly is mangled. "No, Milord, don't be concerned.
I've got one here I tied myself—there's fish yet in that lie."
"You'd better make me up a batch; it's high time that you earned
your tip; the price of flies is so extortionately high."

Steelhead

The steelhead flex, flash copper and flame,
      as they mate in the green-tinged glow.
She tail-scoops gravel, their cradle and grave,
and they spill their life in what passes for love
      among fish, then succumb to the flow.

Washouts are avalanche paths for the slides
      of spates. Uprooted trees sled.
Though eggs from the spawning bed flitter away,
tumble and whiten in colloids of clay,
      new heartbeats stir in the redd.

Under the gravel, the alevins burst
      from roe that were squeezed from the skeins.
With yesterday's instincts innate in each brain
and plenitude primed for their numbers to wane,
      a new generation convenes.

Ingesting their yolk sacs, they flutter. The trout
      enshadow them; herons' quick beaks
chopstick them out as fry and as parr;
some choke—a derailment, a chemicals car—
      and drift, belly up, as it leaks.

Sea otters sentry the river mouth pools
      and ambush them. Smolts in the tide,
they dart, leaving blizzards of scales, then steal
round herring-spawn frenzies of seabird and seal
      to where the Pacific spreads wide.

They linger, adapt to the salt in their gills,
     and, concealed in eelgrass and dulse,
swoop on the ghost shrimp that crawl from the sand
and grow as they wheel in this swift saraband
     till wanderlust quickens their pulse.

They sense low pressure zones scarping the waves
     and the throbs of the freighters that churn
west with their lumber. But humpbacks sing,
and pilot them north on the bow of the spring.
     They follow, and latitudes turn.

The Kodiak Seamount where shearwaters glide
     and geese descend to the floes—
they thrive in its waters where baitfish abound,
and flesh out fully by scale-ring and pound
     in silver, with flanks of faint rose.

A wave, like nostalgia, seems laced with the tang
     of natal creek water, still fresh,
so, shoaling, the cohort's survivors swim home
and weave up the coast through a seine catacomb:
     fish waft, gills flared in the mesh.

A downpour is slanting and slashing across
     the sullen grey board of the sky.
They battle the gauntlets of fishers who cast
before them from jet boats with tackle that's passed
     by guides who have learned where they lie.

The last one living from all of his brood
        arrives at a grand entrance hall
of canyon, then launches through air, spray, and haze,
and flies, his eyes an obsidian blaze,
        scaling each waterfall's wall.

His brain is a diamond that channels the dead.
        He drives as a tuning fork struck
on the steel of a will as relentless as tide;
his muscles pulsate up each torrent and glide,
        propulsions of effort and luck.

In olivine light he crests the last lip,
        the top of the flood's terraced stair;
through headwater bends he fins to that place
of tribulation and trembling and grace;
        a mate of his kind hovers there.

The steelhead flex, flash copper and flame . . .

The Way

The roadway creeps across the contours slowly
and escalates us high above the valley
where, gullied down, the river flows in secret
through falls and logjams. None attempts to drift it
and forests flank its banks—they're steep and rough
with slide-rock gardens, blowdown, bush, and bluff.

We come upon a decommissioned spur road
that leads into the timber, riverwards
through alders thick enough to stop our truck;
we wade its chest-deep brush and feel the track,
invisible below us, rise and fall
through rubble piles and blast-rock stacks until

before us is a citadel. Its face,
blown out by high explosives, forms the base
of logging roads we drove. A played-out quarry.
Water fills its pit, which huckleberry,
salmonberry, devil's club, and thorns
have ringed among the horsetails, banes, and ferns.

Was that a rustle? Cougars must reside
in galleries above. Though we can't hide
from cats whose lives depend on sensing prey,
we walk on, chancing they will stay away
because we look too big to kill with ease;
we're passers-through, observed by eyes in trees.

Mosquitoes whine, a pestilence relieved
by monarch butterflies, which must have weaved
their way from Mexico, and hummingbirds
who shuttlecock their little drinking-swords
from bloom to bloom and sip. Now we're perplexed.
This seems to be a cul-de-sac. Where next?

We bushwhack round the shoulder of the fortress,
and there a hem of bear trail skirts a buttress
above a flood-ripped gorge whose floor is set
with jagged rocks. There is no safety net.
The route dead-ends, but looking off its edge
we see that, lower down, there is a ledge.

We drop and perch above the precipice
then find a keyhole through which we can pass
below the cliff to fallen old-growth timber
and trunks we have to tightrope walk or clamber
over, or, if there is clearance, squirm
beneath and slither, slither, man to worm.

Thus lowly man achieves discoveries
by pressing on, fatigued, on hands and knees
or letting faith and madness shoot the stars
until he reaches realms where, as his ears
hearken to a New World Symphony,
he walks the moon or names the Bering Sea.

And so we come to corridors of light
where radiation fog is now a white
flap of angel wings on morning air

and waters run so clear and pure and bare
we feel we have alighted in a place
where daybreak still distills impalaced grace.

The first surveyors must have walked this course
when charting lands unreachable by horse;
and summer steelhead find their way back here
by leaping falls that thwart the salmon, clear
into this world of ancient trees and pools
and filtered light and wind. And two small fools.

We stalk the tailouts, see the fish and cast
our flies above their lies . . . they float on past,
and even distant steelhead twitch and spook
if we peek up our heads to take a look.
But on occasion we enjoy a splash
and feel a summer steelhead's breakneck dash.

We let them go, unlanded, undefiled,
these silver bullets, offspring of the wild,
unslip our barbless hooks and watch them swim
into the turquoise depths like seraphim
shedding fire in water. Now we know
the way and, cougar-like, may come and go.

Green Hall

I track a tributary corridor
till waters wed, then walk an aisle of green—
      reflecting leaf and conifer,
      the river flows through pools between
      the forest-vaulted valley walls,
      around the bedrock's shoulder-blades,
      along its bouldered balustrades,
      rippling, breaking, till it stalls . . .
      then slips and whitens round a bend
      where canyon flanks and mountains blur
      in heights that leave no room for sky.
      A dipper dips, kingfishers whirr
around a curve where days and decades blend
and seasons tumble reasonlessly by.

October mist scarves air with sea-grey light
and maples drizzle sheens from golden leaves.
      No wind has shaken them to flight,
      to touchdown under dark green weaves
      of ivy in this deep crevasse
      of dripping greens: the salal gleaming
      waxily, the limpid, streaming
      bottle-green beneath the glass
      of glides that slide then smithereen;
      the fern; the lichen's celadon;
      those stalagmites of hunter green—
      the old-growth firs; the low demesne
of chartreuse moss. I brave the current's brawn
in fords where rocks rake rapids like baleen.

Round fragments flung from ice-cracked mountainsides
back eddies burble, opaline and chrome.
    My fly line settles, sinks, and slides
    through lies where steelhead runs have come
    to overwinter till the spring
    then spawn at snow-melt. In the flow
    a surge—it's more than undertow:
    a take that makes my fly reel sing.
    The mist is emerald, enchanted;
    the light is beryl, liquefied,
    the river lucent, moulten jade,
    the rapids nettle tea, decanted.
Mint-green, it swims in view; then I, wide-eyed,
release it to its world and watch it fade.

Wild Immanuel

The pool is basalt black; a charcoal stump
hunkers where I'll fish at morning's glow.
I wait till scouting hints of sunrise jump
the trees, till dawn unblankets dozing snow,
then cast beside the root; lead pocks the gloom
and bellies peeling line around the flanks
of brawling whorls that bound the pewter flume.
I wade around the trees on flooded banks.

The pencil weight strikes bottom, starts to trip:
tic tic. I visualize a contour map:
the riverbed—retrieve, recast, whirr, splip—
in line-tap Braille, and soon I find the lap
in which he'll lie. Below the stump a hollow,
then a rock. Yes, he'll be holding there
balanced on the thalweg, which I follow—
chute, compression wave, and stone-split flare.

Adjust the length of lead. Weight bounce, a knock,
then, scraping down the stone, tic, stop, and strike;
a sense of colossal weight, a moving rock,
followed by slackness. Loss. A thornlike spike
of dorsal fin above a coursing hump—
deep, almost invisible, its arc
sweeps the tailout, slaloms to the stump,
and lets the dawning swallow it like dark.

I watch the patch of water where it sank
then let it float away, with wistfulness;
next day I tramp the meadows to that bank,
where January mist and darkness coalesce.
Today I will be ready when he takes,
alert, prepared to strike him trigger-fast.
Crevasses yawn above the trees—dawn breaks;
this time I know precisely where to cast.

Tic tic, tic tic, tic stop—I've struck already
and now we're locked together; slow pulsations
presage his charge but still he's holding steady;
my instincts wait on his deliberations.
This fish is evolution's masterpiece;
his caudal wrist is thick, his tail is large
to match the Little Qualicum's caprice—
its great, precipitate, flash-flood discharge.

Two hundred times its summer volume—he
can navigate the rapids in that flood,
evading trundling boulders and debris
of trees that spear down through the murk. His blood
begins to surge and urges him to mate,
to pass on traits distinguishable from other
rivers' tribes, to run the winter spate,
he and the torrent steeling one another.

And now he runs, leaves me like Hemingway's
Old Man of the Sea, a throwback Ahab, lost
in crazed resolve. He leaps there in the haze,
spectral, as though flash-frozen by the frost,

then splashes down and disappears inside
his territory of rushing, ice-black water;
he's primed to seek asylum, bolt and hide;
in his world, losing struggles end in slaughter.

He's lost if line guides ice or if he shoots
the glide—a certainty if he otterboards
downstream; the stump's a labyrinth of roots;
upstream the banks are flooded like the fords—
the odds are on his side. I do not dare
to let him choose the duelling ground. I pull
the line; he pulls the strings, goes everywhere—
the windings on my reel reveal the spool.

I let him beat upriver then exert
pressure against him, sideways and downstream
and feel him give; he turns, tries to assert
his course. I have his measure now; abeam,
I let the river sap him, clamber out
beside a grassy cleft lapped by the spate
and, leveraging each thrash, I haul his snout
towards it, slacken off. He lies in state.

I grasp his tail—he offers no resistance—
then kick-pile alder leaves and lay him there,
an altar to our transient coexistence;
red crescents flicker—urgent gill plates flare.
A steelhead buck, raw speed and adrenaline,
quicksilver curves awash over ochre and cream,
eye wilder than his unclipped adipose fin,
at twenty pounds, he's a trophy hunter's dream.

But not for me. In truth I am relieved;
such saviours of the wild gene pool are blessed
with mandatory release. He is reprieved.
I float him, breathing, till he kicks to wrest
himself from my supporting sling of hands
through icy water. His back is long and green
as he propels himself to hinterlands
of winter-runs in the river's cold ravine.

And in some cloud of flittering gravel he
released the milt of millennial design
alongside hatchery does; then recently
the run did not return—a broken line.
But still I walk the meadowland and see
his first and second comings in the mist—
his sacred fin, his leap, him swimming free,
that final wave of tail and caudal wrist.

To the Dead of Winter

Little Qualicum River, after the fall salmon run

Now is the time of the moss
and it blankets the alders en masse
as they stand in the mists of the bottomland;
though witch's hair drapes from their frames
they're but haggard old widows in weeds
who abide by the graves of your race,
  for these trees seem so sere that their sap will not rise,
  that their laceworks of leaves will not lattice the skies
  though their greyness and gauntness have donned the disguise
of these snow-sprinkled greensleeves of fleece.

Now is the time of the snow
though at noon there's a moment of thaw
when the river runs clear by the skulls
and the gill plates at rest in the shallows
or enveloped in white on the gravel
like masks. And your head has a jaw
  that grew hooked as you ran with your instincts aflame
  and your scales turning scarlet; the maples became
  inflamed with your fire, which the winter would tame
as it laid down your dead like the law.

Now is the time of the dead
between fall, when the fleshpots were red,
and the frenzy of feeding that spring
will bring with the fingerling fry—

they will die in the dance of the riffle
or flee to the redds in the bed
      from mergansers, and herons, and gulls to endure
      as their myriads falter to fewer and fewer
      till they run for the sea and return when mature
to this boneyard, from which they were bred.

Now is the time of the bones,
of your petrified gape. It bemoans
how the beaks picked your skeleton clean
as they pecked out your stomach and heart
through a grille-work of ventricle racks
on a spine that is chevroned with spines,
      leaving teeth that ripped herring-balls—blood, scale, and skin,
      leaving orbits your eyeballs were gimballed within
      and an arrowhead neb that was driven by fin
to be bonded by ice to these stones.

Now is the time of the bonds,
of the destinies twined like the fronds
in the lichen. Your whole generation,
who hailed from this valley, returned
and in thousands engaged in an orgy,
its climax a Slough of Despond's
      sh-sh-shudder as victims were swallowed—the strife
      as the spawning stress killed with its gralloching knife
      and you wallowed in currents that vied for your life,
with which Time, the great river, absconds.

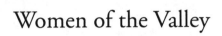

Women of the Valley

River Woman

Did you ever fall in love with a river
and feel her sinews slide across the land?
Did her undercurrents ever make you quiver
    and suck you down and down
    through breathless dreams to drown
in turbulence of bubbles and glistening sand?

Is she the wild Stikine or Tatshenshini,
is she the summer-silked Similkameen,
is she the lithe, long-legended Homathko,
are her eyes the glacier melting turquoise-green?

Did you ever let her flowing sweep you downstream
and lose your stone-held footing in the spate?
Did she flush you through a canyon on a sunbeam,
    sluice raceways through your mind,
    careen you fast and blind,
then glide you down her pools, now so sedate?

Were you ever cradled softly in her valley,
borne on a straining sheet of shining light,
turned slowly in a silent, swan-like ballet,
    rocks sliding by below,
    the land an upstream flow,
your mind a swirling haze of green and white?

Yes, she's the wild Stikine and Tatshenshini.
Yes she's the summer-silked Similkameen.
Yes she's the lithe, long-legended Homathko.
Her eyes are the glacier melting, turquoise-green.

Women of the Ages

I'm the lass of Invergarry,
singing by the loch alone
of the lad I was to marry,
of the baby in my belly
he begot but would not own.

I'm the mother of Glenfinnan,
feeding sons who gird and go,
dreading battles, ripping linen,
dressing wounds and watching crimson
drench the strips of my trousseau.

I'm the widow of Culloden,
sowed and reaped and left to weeds
till I'm winter-tilled and sodden,
till my tilth and clods are broken
by the cold that kills my seeds.

We're the women of the ages,
wooed to walk the aisles of grief;
we're the wear on well-worn pages
where posterity retraces
deeds of men in bold relief.

Woman in the Wind

Sheets of rusted corrugated iron
clatter in the gusts against its walls,
the black house mossed with memories of childhood—
it passed like sunset blushed across the kyles.
A teenage bride, she wed her next-door neighbour;
one gateway and she crossed her line of blood.
Today, that field gate lies unhinged and fallen,
half sunk in a half a lifetime's puddled mud
and only washing line connects the gate posts.
Three shirts with arms extended tug and flap—
a man, two boys. She sees three crucifixions
and thinks of all the prayers and benedictions
they've counted on to save them from mishap.

    Their rowboat rounds the Cregan to the Sound
    of Raasay out of Camustianavaig Bay.
    Black cormorants, like mourners, watch them pass
    behind Ben Tianavaig, then fade away.
    At tide change there's a hush as waters still.
    Red cod in congregations prey and gulp
    the eels that undulate like blowing rags
    as handlines search their sanctuaries of kelp.
    Clouds glisten, haloed by a hidden sun.
    The brightness weakens to the creak of oars.
    Then wingless shadows fly across the heather,
    grey waves of swelling rain bring foul weather
    as storms begin to sweep the open moors.

This morning and each morning since she married
she's borne the water buckets from the burn
to wash away the woad of savage living
expecting neither respite nor return.
From unrelenting slime and sweat and smearings,
she keeps the gate, defies the coming squall,
extracts the wind's last spitless drying breath;
but now both rain and iron rattle the wall.
In headscarf, tallowed boots, and threadbare coat
she wears for milking and when going for peat
she pulls the clothes-pegs, hoping that it brightens;
instead the cowl of gloom draws in and tightens,
and rain spots on the clothes seal her defeat.

    Now serried whitecaps charge the assembled leagues
    of shoreline cliffs then crash like cracks of doomsday
    and rise as giant clamshells on the rocks;
    though bow to blow, four oars can make no headway.
    They slash their grounded lines and blisters tear
    from callused hands as limbs and torsos, wood—
    one streaming sinewed beast impelled by fear—
    resist the pounded Cregan's beatitude.
    No bell, just stony silence from the kirk
    where ministers tell all they're unforgiven
    until they die, then say they've gone to Heaven,
    cold comfort as the combers go berserk.

She steps inside and fights to shut the door.
Outside the ravens huddle under haystacks,
and seagulls switchback into battering gales.
The iron sheeting flies. She finds some sacks

and caulks the drafty door, then lifts the wash
and squeezes hard to feel if it's still moist
with water hauled before her menfolk rose;
then grasps these family icons to her breast,
damp armfuls of limp empty cloth, and knows,
as surely as the sun will set forever
beyond the kyles, as surely as the kirk
will keep its foregone verdicts under cover,
that, whether she must face a widow's grief,
or they return expecting her relief,
until she dies, one of two Hells awaits her.

Hay

In communal harvest, I swing my scythe smoothly
from hay swathe to hay swathe. The village wave washes
the crofts of the valley. You hay-wade here blithely.
As commonfolk harvest, I swing my scythe smoothly.
You bend as you winnow out weeds, pulling lithely.
My scythe blade is silver; it limberly swishes.
In communal harvest, I swing each sweep smoothly
from hay swathe to hay swathe. The village wave washes.

You work with the women. You do not look my way.
Bent cailleachs bring cloths full of crowdie and oatcake.
I cast my glance your way to see what your eyes say—
you work with the women, you do not look my way.
Back bending, breasts cradled, your smile glimmers shyly.
They hope you have learned all the weeds that make cows sick,
the women you work with. I see them look my way,
the cailleachs with cloths full of crowdie and oatcake.

I know you are longing for my eyes to meet yours.
Last night we awaited the cusp of the gloaming
to slip from our houses and make for the peat moors;
we knew we were longing for my lips to meet yours.
We followed the burnside and swayed with its detours
then gazed on the sea waves, their silver light gleaming
and lingered in longing as my fingers clasped yours
last night when we crested the cusp of the gloaming.

As deep as the bedrock our hearts beat together;
the soughing breeze laved us in night-breath communion.
The old sheep enclosure of dry stone and heather
delivered the bed where our hearts beat together,
a haunting cathedralled tattoo through the machair.
A sod seat for shearing was bed for our union—
there, deep as the bedrock our hearts beat together
as breeze's sighs laved us in night-breath communion.

You work here so close to my whet-stoned edge melting
the thistledown hay. Our secret is soul-bound
and yet there's deep slicing, and yet there's sad lilting
as we work so closely, my whet-stoned edge melting
the soft-falling sheaves. I saw your eyes misting
in trust and in tryst on the high folding hill ground.
You work there so close to my whet-stoned edge melting
the thistledown hay. Our secret is soul-bound.

The Call of the Wild

I lie a little late luxuriating
in stretchiness from yesterday's dawn run
around the island with the eastern sun
igniting rose hips and accentuating

the crimson of arbutus limbs. I cruise
down to the bakery for new-baked bread
and freshly ground Colombian. Ahead
of me in line two goddesses enthuse

about the prospect of a swim. *The dock
at Graham Lake is best, and so serene,*
the server says, *that after you have been
no other lake will do. But please don't talk*

for it's a secret. Wink. They smile, say *Thanks.*
I take my coffee to the shore and chat
with coho fishermen, discover that
the fish are in. Tonight, I'll join their ranks

but to the cabin now; from there I see
the mermaids naked on the dock, both flinging
their hair backwards and forwards, laughter ringing
across the lilies, inhibition-free.

My handsome rowboat with the wineglass stern
lies moored and waiting and my fly rod's near;
I could go fishing and make it appear
coincidence that I catch them, discern

their frolicking in this secluded spot.
Perhaps they'll need a place that's warm and dry
after their September dip? And why
does adolescence still afflict my thought?

I buck a cord of firewood, autumn's chore,
and wonder if the water nymphs are gone,
restrain myself. I must resist being drawn
to Loreleis we boatmen should ignore

so I give other matters precedence
and plant spring-flowering bulbs, a small surprise
to cheer my wife and family—I'm wise
to which of nature's impulses make sense.

Then to the shore. The twilight water's mauve
and sea lions tail-slap somewhere in the strait;
as darkness falls the shallows seethe with bait—
I hear the *splats* of coho in the cove . . .

a strike! The line rips off my reel and, *hiss*,
it slices through the water like a shark fin,
raises a rooster tail, a jagged mark in
the avenue of moonlight; I almost miss

the swerve towards me, swift as a bolting hare,
but I retrieve the slack, wade to some shelves
where fish can be seduced to beach themselves.
A hen, she lies there, gasping, as I stare

before I loose her to her place of birth,
the ephemeral creek that calls her to redeem
the generation that, with ample beam,
she cargos deep within her glistening girth.

Like her, I sense the press of ancient urges
to run, to hunt and mate, and now to kill—
they lace my blood but can't dissolve my will;
she's free. There's evolution in her surges

and night is falling; dusk unrolls a sea fog
and tucks it round the islands like a parent
keeping its charges safe from threats it daren't
contemplate. The croaking of a tree frog

calls me ashore where cloven woods reveal
the road—I drive dark palisades where deer
emerge like woodland ghosts then disappear.
Inside I cook a solitary meal:

with thanks to Windy Marsh Organic Farm,
a hearty soup; bread from the bakery trip;
and silence—only the water container's drip,
its audibility an island charm . . .

until the barred owl ululates to me—
wooh-ooh-ah-ooh, wooh-ooh, wooh-ooh-ah-ooh—
inviting me to form a choir of two.
The woodstove winks, sufficient intimacy

for comfort as I go to bed alone
and think of how my family will come
tomorrow night and make this place a home.
Though wilder worlds may call, I like my own.

My Nokomis

From the full moon fell Nokomis,
Fell the beautiful Nokomis
    — "The Song of Hiawatha," Longfellow

Our solar orbits calibrate the ages
and graduate our lives—years, each distinct,
frame annals where our lore and loves are linked,
but lunar months illuminate the pages.

On silver nights, the highlights of each season
gave elders ways of looking at full moons,
not just as discs, celestial picayunes,
but as personae, cast there for a reason.

Like you, the same but ever changing: *Wolf,*
Hunger, Crust, Fish, Flower, Strawberry, Buck,
Sturgeon, Harvest, Hunter, Beaver, Cold,
rich calendars that overspan the gulf
from when we met to now, where I'm still struck
by light from your corona of white gold.

A Many-Splendoured Thing?

Is love a beaming, eye to eye? An oath—*you-only-till-I-die?*
A U that comes before an I? A hullabaloo-cum-lullaby?
A flirt? A tilting of the neck? An art? A Machu Picchu trek
back in time to that valiant peck on virgin cheek, that *what-the-heck?*

A brace of lovebirds who embrace instead of pecking cheeks, a plaice
whose eyes achieve a state of grace—as one on one side of its face?
A willing ear we learn to ration between soliloquies? A fashion?
The winning chips we hope to cash in from laying on the wheel of passion?

A bridle? Or a bridal dress? An *if-you-love-me-you'll . . .* duress?
A scandal in the gutter press? A *touch-me-there-uh-huh* caress?
A smile without the crow's-feet creases? A summer fling that never ceases?
A joining of two jigsaw pieces? A joke? A yoke with quick-releases?

Love grins with its beret askew, climbs up the sky and paints it blue
then turns the sun to shine on you and says, *"You're puzzled? Hey, me too!"*

Request for a Dance

Step with me, float with me, over the floor;
weave with me, waltz with me, out through the door;
slide to the deck where the crowdedness clears;
glide through the garden and tear off your fears.

Step with me, sneak with me, down to the lake,
onto its waters; the mirror won't break;
lilt in a ball gown of luminous mist;
twirl till you're breathless and need to be kissed.

Step with me, skim with me, let yourself go,
dazzling and dizzy, then flowingly slow;
whirl till our swirls make a maelstrom of night;
pass through the portal from here to delight.

Step with me, sway with me, feel yourself swing,
hammocked on rhythms of hearts on the wing;
move to the measures of seasons and years;
sweep to that island where time disappears.

Step with me, slip with me, up to its crypt,
quaff a last laugh from the pleasures we've sipped;
curtsey and smile at a parting of hands
joined in this dancing by two wedding bands.

Echoes

Immortal Memory

for Robert Burns

The twenty-fifth of January,
1759 AD,
brings you into this world, a wee
     and helpless bairn,
as Scotland's hope stands hopelessly:
     Culloden's cairn.

You live on farms and grow up poor
in penuries that fast inure
men to the plough and stony moor
     to scrape a living
from land few farmers can endure—
     harsh, unforgiving.

And yet you find small ways to heed
the beauty of that land, to read
its books, its lines, its lore, its breed
     of common people
buckled beneath the crushing creed
     of laird and steeple.

Your nineteenth birthday—now you link
the joy of words, the work of drink;
you make Tarbolton Inn-mates think
     in what you dub
to be a common man's—clink, clink—
     debating club.

And you rebel, your sword the pen,
wielded with fiery acumen,
and beard the lions in their den—
     the church and gentry—
in bold defence of working men,
     their saint and sentry.

You raise the cotter's head up high,
compare drunk Tam to kings and try
false Holy Willie for his lie;
     you claim the clan
of humans is ennobled by
     the honest man.

Young women worship what you say
and lie with you in summer hay
then bear your brood the following May
     when you can't stop
the cultivation, then in play
     for next year's crop.

So many loves to kiss, enthrall,
and catch as in your arms they fall—
you portion solace to them all
     with vows in songs
that part of you, on some fair knoll,
     to each belongs.

But in the end it's death you fight—
lost infants, loves, your body's blight—
and, as you do, you write and write

throughout your strife
and universalise the plight
        of burning life.

No man can tether time or tide
so off on Tam's grey mare you ride
across Hell's barren countryside
        where you compose
a song of hope and plant with pride
        one red, red rose.

Rab, look at what you've left behind—
a nation's heritage defined
by peopled landscapes of the mind;
        we laud your birth
as yet your old Scots verses bind
        the world's worth.

A Sweetness Absent from the Ocean Air

The Weeping Window bleeds ceramic poppies
that blush St. Magnus's cathedral wall
and each seems minuscule among them all—
the throng comprises nigh a million copies:
one bloom per British serviceman who died
in World War One, a massive flower bed
entitled *Blood Swept Lands and Seas of Red*
displayed in London where it dignified
that War's centenary. Now part has travelled
to Orkney, here to mark one century
since dreadnought fleets waged battle on the sea
near Jutland. Lifelines tangled and unravelled—
in two short days eight thousand men and more
succumbed as riven battleships went down.
With Princess Anne, the envoy of the Crown,
their relatives are welcomed at the door
of this, the Viking edifice erected
in memory of Magnus, who eschewed
bad blood in favour of the holy rood,
a man of peace, nine hundred years respected.

Some families take pause and stare, as if
they hope the flower avatar of their
lost sailor lad will wave. As they repair
into the church, the poppies stand up, stiff
like soldiers at attention on parade;
their stems are wire, their heads are crimson clay
and, grouped, they seem ethereal, a fey

honour guard shipshapedly displayed.
The British and the German brass bands march
along the harbour front, then through the streets;
this day there are no triumphs or defeats—
they gain the church grounds through a common arch—
and then the pipe band, clad in kilts, assemble.
No instrument of war can so foment
bravado, then bestow such dark lament:
Great Highland bagpipes set the air atremble,
the Weeping Window work of art revives,
more vehemently, the ones who drowned and bled,
and now we see, in child-tall blooms of red,
a sad cascade of young, foreshortened lives.

The Burn of Hallaig

On the Island of Raasay you can walk to Hallaig, a crofting village that was
cleared for sheep. A burn runs through a wood there and ends in a waterfall that
falls from a cliff to the shore. On a cairn overlooking the old fields and ruined
walls you can read, in English and in Gaelic, the greatest Gaelic poem of our time,
"Hallaig" by the late Sorley MacLean. I spent summers as a boy in the crofting
village of Camustianavaig in Braes, where my father was raised. Camustianaviag
Bay looked across to Raasay. Sorley retired to Braes, died there, and is buried in
Aros, outside Portree, in the same graveyard as my father, other members of our
family, and other villagers from Camustianavaig.

Time, that fell with the deer, is in the moving water of burns
    as it catches the leaves that are fallen too early for autumn.
In Camustianavaig's Bay, for as long as can be remembered,
    a MacDonald here, a Nicholson there, a Bain,
a Beaton, a MacLean like yourself, would be drawn by the burn and drifted
    to Kyle or Glasgow, to Chicago or Santiago,
        leaving the islands, famined for fortune.

You'll have seen that burn on your way to your final home in Braes.
    I would hear its water in the mornings and know by its sound
if a rain had come in the night. And you'll know the house whose track
    is a sickle on the hill. It's a road I know by its building—
as boys, young Neil and I, with our father, and big Neil, his brother,
    worked long, drawing its base from the house's hill-cut,
        and gazing to the point of Peinachorran

and beyond, as the Cuillins stood and changed with the light from black
    as the spring tar on the boats, to mauve and green
and airy grey, while the teeth of the Sgurrs tore at the clouds.
    To the east, Raasay breached like a whale of rock,
and I never knew then that, as the sun segued to moonlight,

you may have been over below Dun Caan, watching
        the pines wind-tossed on Cnoc an Ra.

Your gift of words makes me think of you this Sunday, Sorley,
        as I walk to Hallaig on the path that runs from Fearns.
The bracken here is bog-green. In a place where a field could be,
        it breaks on a lichened dyke that was made of stones
from the clearing of land for people. I look down at seagulls
        wheeling below, as once you looked from a Cuillin,
            perched above the Corrie of Solitude,

and saw below you an eagle, golden, the Skye bird, then wrote
        that it glimmered with glory. Today the gulls have the white
of lighthouses, and the prawn buoys, pink as salmon eggs,
        cork on a windless sea that must always be watched.
At length I come to your cairn, where the words of your poem are written
        in your own Gaelic, and in your own English, cut
            into plates of brass on wind-polished stone.

With its lines in my ears like the sea sound in shells, I walk the path
        by the birches like girls, by the burn, by your love, the rowan,
and catch the cadence of their moving in the Gaelic of the stream
        till, again, the woods come alive with the endless walk.
But there's no beginning here. And, drawn by water, I move
        downstream and past where the path rises to the hill
            then set my boots at the top of a cliff.

For the slope of the burn through the woods, that was gentle and gave it its
    pools
        and its tripping steps in the safe enclave of the trees,
            has stopped.

Back at the cairn I see, for the first time, the waterfall.
     It breaks on the rocks as you lie in the Aros graveyard,
as do my parents and big Neil who, without child of his own,
     taught young Neil the ways of working the land,
and as does young Neil's wife, who left him with children, a widower.
     For want of a living in Skye he will lose the croft,
       which others in Aros hayed as a village.

When I stood above that fall, I could hear the water and tell
     that the island rains had been heavy. One Monday morning
in eighteen fifty-four, Rainy, for that was his name,
     had thirty-seven evicted and sent to Australia,
to storms and typhus from the only home they'd ever known—
     and that loss of a croft that has passed between generations
       takes only the sounds of the gulls and the Gaelic.

As your flesh departs the bone, like the people departing Hallaig,
     the Gaelic you gave us in English echoes like a coronach
and on this windswept Sunday your words cry sorely, Sorley,
     across the land where the deer lies dead of love,
retelling the tale of this place and the trees that walk by the burn,
     and of all the burns that ever were, the Great Tale—
       your sermon on the Sabbath of the dead.

For the Crofters

My ancestors, you were burned from the glens

As the ice gouged Strathcarron, then melted to mingle with sea-loch, you
    melted from glens to the shore.

When your roof-timbers crackled in Sutherland's fires at Strathnaver, you
    scoured a treeless coastline.

As the fall of the wind-sand made machair by Luskintyre's Sound, you
    blew and shifted and settled.

When the factors staked crofts on scraps of blasted Strathy, you thrashed
    in the grip of the gusts.

and built on the coast.

As the sandstone sediments buried each other in Caithness, you split
    them and built with the flagstone.

While your clachan surrendered to moss at Achanlochy, you coursed new
    walls in the wind.

As the mica sparkled from Moine schist slabs in Argyll, your lintels and
    byre stalls glittered.

As whale bones braced Stone-Age roofs at Skara Brae, you thatched your
    rafters with marram.

You broke the bleakness of the land,

As the runrigs still wrap the ruins of Auchindrain, your townships were
    plaids for the bays.

As the Vikings sculpted their pots from the soapstone of Unst, you hand-
    ploughed your fields from the moor.

As gneiss cupped pools of rainfall that brimmed with sphagnum, you
 sustained the peat-fire flame.
When the spring brought transhumance and high-ground grazing for cattle,
 you husbanded low ground for crops.

farmed it,

As the Standing Stones of Callanish jut from the earth, your seedlings
 sprouted in spring.
As Mousa's broch builders ground their grain in querns, you milled the bere
 for your bannocks.
When the black-faced sheep grazed the outby scattalds of Flugarth, you
 drove them in with your dogs.
As pilasters of basalt kilted the cliffs of Staffa, you wore the wool that you
 spun.

and harvested the sea.

As the Ness men row to Sula Sgeir for gugas, you climbed for the eggs of the
 guillemot.
As the meltwater gouged Corrieshalloch to shelter the sanicle, you dug
 nousts in the shore for your boats.
As the Bronze Age people of Jarlshof filled middens with fishbone, you
 trammelled the silver darlings.
As Fingal's Cave mouthed its Hebridean wind-songs, you rowed on the
 swells with Mendelssohn.

But hunger came nonetheless.

As the rain hollowed caves at Smoo and Assynt from limestone, your bellies
 were hollowed by winter.
While the seaweed burned in the kelp fire kilns of the Uists, you laboured
 for lairds who starved you.

As the planticrues fed the people of Shetland with cabbage, you bent your
    backs on potatoes.
When the blight blown from Ireland blackened the haulms of your hope, you
    ate nettles and shellfish and weeds.

You coped as you could,

When Macleod of Dunvegan doled bolls of meal for your thralldom, you
    prayed for the faerie flag.
When Cromarty's laird built a Gaelic church to tempt you, your sweat
    anointed his fortunes.
When the Lothian fields and the Glasgow factories lured you, you walked the
    length of the nation.
While the lairds of Lewis and Barra evicted the starving, you paid your rent
    with your flesh.

and many left forever.

When MacDonald deported three generations from Suishnish, your wails
    were a funeral coronach.
When the lowly lairded the wilds of Nova Scotia, you waved to your children
    from wharves.
When the Ballarat gold-rush siphoned Australia's labour, your neighbours
    followed old felons.
While Lord Selkirk settled the land-locked Red River prairie, you waited for
    unwritten letters.

You remained and fought

When orphans returned on ships turned back with typhus, you shared your
    meagre shelter.
When the women of Braes stoned constables sent from Glasgow, you turned
    an ancient tide.

When the rent protesters of Glendale were jailed in Edinburgh, you
unsheathed the steel of the martyr.

When the cottars fought the gunboat marines at Aignish, you defied the
feudal fist.

for reform.

When Lord Napier's Commission listened in the Ollach Schoolhouse,
your wielded your words like broadswords.

When your spokespeople told how women and men pulled harrows, you
bridled the brutish factors.

When the laird of Kirkwall blackballed those who bore witness, you
braved his retribution.

When the nation's conscience adopted the Crofting Act, you secured your
rights of tenure.

You made your living for a time,

While last century's waves unrolled on the beaches of Harris, your lives
rolled, poor and proud.

As you walked by Sligachan into the mists of the Cuillins, you worked,
and the world slid by.

While the march of progress became a battle charge, you nurtured your
land by the decade.

As the ages changed the shapes of the Shetland voes, your time-honoured
ways eroded.

and changed with the times.

While Lorgill, the glen of the deer's cry, lay deserted, you moved from the
old black houses.

As the lords of the lambs paid a guinea a dead golden eagle, you traded
your garrons for tractors.

As the drovers swam cattle across Kylerhea's swift narrows, you bridged the sea to Skye.

As you drive on the roads that run where your forefathers trod, you lean to the whine of the wind.

Creekwalker

*for Ian McAllister, a man dedicated to the preservation of the Great
Bear Rainforest*

He jogs the hopscotch patches worn to the earth
through tree-frog greens and sunlight spears and sparks
where grizzlies yield fawn lilies careful berth,
confining their paws to these well-trodden marks

that stitch the forest. And now he sees the ripple,
the splash, the whorl, the familiar wallowing
where fins and tails of the spawning salmon stipple
the glare. He's spent a lifetime following

this valley to the creek's headwaters where
it plunges from its flume of mountain granite,
a cataract descending in a flare
of mare's tails from the cloud stream that began it.

And other creeks on both sides of the fjord,
are his—he must patrol them, count, and report;
the Fisheries Department cannot afford
its data stream of hindsight to fall short

of inundating prudence. He was raised
in Bella Bella where the Heiltsuk Nation,
campaigning to save one valley, watch, amazed,
as others succumb to clear-cut desolation.

The numbers he has registered down the years,
plain as the petroglyphs, relate their stories—
runs dwindling as his lifespan shrinks. He fears
they'll go the way of the cod and the Grand Banks dories

before his grandsons even open their eyes,
that they'll never see a ghost-white spirit bear.
Though ten Yosemites cannot match its size
he's worried for the Great Bear Rainforest where

the wolf packs course like combers through the night
while cougars glide along the limbs of cedars
and orca pods disperse to assault each bight
and inlet, synchronised, conducted by leaders

attuned instinctively to the seasonal drum
that beats to the massings of herring, sockeye, and pink
and, to seal-slap percussion, chinook and coho and chum
by river mouth and run time. Now the chink

of chains is signalling that a logging load
is readied for the booming grounds and the sea.
He watches the truck mud-bombing down the road,
and then unsheathes his record book where he

keeps tallies of these trips, of how they increase,
beside his log of the salmon runs' decline,
the balance sheet of force-inflicted peace—
he turns towards the cedars, sensing a sign

like eagles, thousand-fold, he once saw craze
the seas of silvery eulachon shoals for oil
or the sedge grass bursting, billiard table baize,
over estuaries where grizzlies root the soil—

a whiteness condenses among the moss and boughs
and slowly a spirit bear becomes manifest
and stands in the roseate light, then turns and ploughs
through salmon redds towards the reddening west.

To the Bluenose

With a hundred and forty feet of hull
       and a quarter acre of sail,
you'd forge up under four lowers against
       head seas in a fifty-knot gale
with a ballast load of Atlantic cod
       and, pitching to the rail,
you'd stand on, with the strength of a church
       and the heft of a breaching whale.

And never had such a spectacle graced
       the Nova Scotian coast
as your flying jib off Lunenberg.
       It was Canada's pride and a boast
that our great salt banker could fly as fleet
       as an ice-filled Gloucester ghost;
and you'd lead round the high-flyer poles, then surf
       wing and wing to the finishing post.

But the price of the cod was crosstree high—
       to harvest your Grand Banks quarry
you'd launch and loose your flying sets
       and, with flambeaux lit, each dory
would anchor a mile of baited line
       as its crew hallooed in the hoary
vapours that rolled from Labrador.
       Then they'd lead-line for death or glory.

They that go down to the sea in ships
      is inscribed on the Man at the Wheel
in Gloucester to mourn the five thousand drowned
      in filling a continent's creel.
And in Lunenberg Harbour twelve hundred names more
      are dancing a stony reel
in a compass of pillars. If ever they rise,
      may they climb with your top men and feel
your halyards thrum and your backstays strain
      on the breakers of Banquereau
as you close-haul with a bone in your teeth
      and your weather bilge bared to the blow.

The Sea

Daybreak, Tofino

The sand is of doeskin, the mizzle is bright
for the sun is a lamp above sleepwalking mist,
and the land intermingles with dimness—the night
still lingers, asleep on the rainforest's chest,
       but is slipping away
       in a luminous grey
from the hills and the headlands that hammock the bay
       as its forehead is kissed
         by the light.

Each wave is an indigo ripple on slate,
which advances, glissando, a wraith from a wall
of nothingness, makes the expanse undulate
like the wandering remnant of some perfect squall,
       then swells to a ledge
       that is stropped to an edge
by the whet of the wind, and collapses to sledge
       up the foreshore with all
         of its freight.

In frothing white crescents they scallop the strand
with dazzling magnesium fire in the haar
and flare through the sea fog until they have fanned
themselves out, then they ebb away leaving no scar
       as the veils of grey clear
       and the capes reappear
and, a ghost in the background, the form of a deer
       manifests on the far
         doeskin sand.

In Living Colour

From parting seas, the grey's great knuckled back,
where barnacles and orange whale lice ride,
rises like a headland, mottled hide
distressed with scar-patched scratches. The Zodiac
planes in. Its watchers gasp—the behemoth
bows to plumb the pools of aquamarine
sand, to siphon shrimps through combs of baleen;
its tail flukes slip from boils of whorls and froth.

An orca's dorsal sets the second scene—
a whale in black and white, an exhibition
of contrasts limned in balanced composition.
Another, another, another, crumpling the green
veneer—cameras swing and click, give chase;
a sea lion breaches, red, with half a face.

Elementary Education

It's cold. Wind sweeps these islands, sea to peak,
across their stiffened fur of frosted trees;
as chill seeps down my leg—my waders leak—
my upwind, ungloved hand begins to freeze.
      And there's the otter.

He disappears. A pluck! The fish has fled.
At last my smolt-like fly aroused attack,
a snap that hit behind the hook. Instead
of blaming karma I should clip it back.
      And there's the otter.

He takes a breather, flips, and slips beneath
the chop, whose whitecaps scrabble at my waist
yip-yapping that, with lethal claws and teeth,
he's captured almost every fish he's chased.
      Again the otter.

A splash. A school of cutthroat trout? A pull.
My line goes slack. I knew that fly would fail.
The master glares—*Attend your inner school*—
duck-dives, and ends the lesson with his tail.
      And there's the water.

Close to Coho

Dawn

I walk the beach by light of predawn stars,
discern the creek and track its shoreline swale
along a trace where rocks and gravel meet
and shells lie still as ivory in graves.
The tide is low and freshly off the turn.
I note a surface seam, fresh water's trail.

And through the silver dulse weed at its mouth
I wade to level sandy-bottomed ground.
The eelgrass lies in patches, swaying east:
the tide begins to move along the coast,
and salmon schools align to face its flow;
I've judged that here a shoal will swing around.

I cast my fly into the sun's first blush.
A morning breeze begins to grate its sheen,
and then I see a single coho jump,
full clear and fresh above that steely seam.
And nothing happens after that, no fish
shows elsewhere in this panoramic scene.

Dusk

I stand in broad salt water to my waist
as sunset fires the mainland crags like coals;
mergansers dive for bait fish, smooth as lead,

and coho leap to greet October skies;
their spangling splashes ring the mirrored sea;
they spring and slap, high spirited as foals.

I see a racing bulge, I'm in its path,
a bolting coho flashes into view;
it barrels breakneck to the shallow shore,
careening past, a yard from my two legs;
its chevroned wake humps by, I feel the sway,
and then the sea before me breaks in two.

About to collide, the sea lion skids to a turn
and whorls the water hugely where I wade;
his flipper rudders strain to turn his bulk
from plunging on at closing killing speed;
upsurges gurgle as he arcs, submerged.
I stand, a one-man save-the-fish stockade.

Killing a Coho

West coast of Vancouver Island

I grip its tail, hammock its back,
and swing its head down with a crack
on rock, then feel its spasms judder
through my hands as, with a shudder,
                    it stills,
            a finale that fulfils
some ancient impulse in my mind.

Poking my finger through a gill,
I cause the raker fronds to spill
blood that drip-drips as I carry
the silver deadweight of my quarry,
                    my kill,
            towards a tidal pool
the sunset has incarnadined.

My knife begins behind its throat
and blood clouds billow out and bloat
then seep into an outflow, seawards,
where baitfish burrow in the seaboard
                    in schools,
            their heads in sand, small fools
kidding themselves they're hard to find.

I slit its stomach. From that sac
their half-digested eyes peer back,
sandlance dumbstruck at being hunted

in shallow flats this prowler haunted,
                    this fish
            whose every feeding flash
signalled flesh to seals behind.

Somewhere nearby a black bear roars;
wolves salivate; an antler gores
a starving cougar; orcas cripple
humpbacks, bite their fins, then grapple
                    great bulks
            till bleeding, savaged hulks
sink; and then there's humankind.

No kindness here. This salmon swam
full speed to seize my lure then, *wham*,
became a madcap, hell-for-leather,
death-row inmate on a tether
                    and fed
            the caveman in my head.
This coast is one big hunting blind.

Siren of the Sea Cliffs

Siren in the salal hurdling nurse logs.
Yet again, this nightmare! Unawake,
fooled by dreamworld fraud, I feel I'm rising.
Through the door I hear the breakers break.

Howling on the sea wind there's a she-wolf
calling to me as she does each night.
Huntress, now my hauntress, are you here to
make my conscience leap at me and bite?

Now I feel I'm walking to the seashore
drawn against my will by déjà vu—
here our children gathered low-tide mussels,
till that day, un-terrorised by you.

Years ago, when kayaking, we saw your
cubs play hide-and-seek in cedar roots,
driftwood logs, and salt-marsh salicornia,
cute as house-raised puppy malamutes.

Silver-furred and sloe-eyed, you would howl from
outcrop rocks as if proclaiming grief
so we called you Siren of the Sea Cliffs,
ululating sound to swathe a reef.

I, like you, competed for my bedmate,
flirting as the dance hall boys drank beers
till my man prey dumped a dull Dolores,
cheap mascara blackening her tears.

We came here to homestead where storm-conquered
fence posts, ploughs, and sea dykes spoke of failed
Scandinavian settlers. Dovetail-jointed
ruins lay abandoned—lives unnailed.

Undeterred, we built a driftwood cabin.
Effort made it windproof, watertight,
woodstove warm and cosy in the winter,
strong, and safe from wildlife in the night.

Even so, we clashed with you. Whenever,
seeking food, my husband set a snare,
you and your companions poached his captures;
all you spared for us was blood and hair.

Presently we found your hidden den mouth—
ravens overhead signposted that.
Squawking, they would pilot you to quarry,
watch you eat, then land and dine on scat.

Once, when you'd gone hunting prey, my husband
watched your cave, as, bolting from its door,
sentries tore a blundering bear to pieces,
ripping it to lumps of fur and gore.

Soon we came to know your daily circuits,
paw prints stamped on earth by pack stampedes;
we were cautious, keeping well away from
paths that linked your killing sites like beads:

Humboldt squid marooned in ancient fish traps;
haul-outs pillowed wall to wall with seals;
riverfuls of salmon, otters, beavers;
herons, cranes, and crabs for lesser meals.

Autumn offered salmon runs. We shared them.
Alder branches smoked our coho meat.
You, with your carnassial teeth, snipped off their
heads and crunched them—skulls were all you'd eat.

Winter was a challenge. You couldn't carry
forward food from times of plenty nor
hibernate like grizzlies. You still had to
feed your needy, inner carnivore.

Cold months thus demanded feral focus—
deer herds would collect in snow-free glades
under forest canopies to forage,
narrowing the reaches of your raids.

Deer were scarce one year. You changed your pattern,
turning on a January day
to the shore and making for our children.
Screams announced your surge into the bay.

Yipping, closing fast, you launched the kill charge:
tails erect as war staffs, on you stormed,
guard hairs at full bristle. Panic-stricken,
I reacted as our kids were swarmed.

Leveling my husband's hunting rifle,
I took aim and dropped your alpha mate.
You and your marauders sniffed the body;
we retrieved our children while you ate.

Watching while your death squad ripped and ravened,
windigos who gorged on fellow meat,
I no longer thought your yowling mournful—
grief took second place when you could eat.

That was when I knew I must be ruthless,
overcome all thought of bad and good,
tell my husband what to do, becoming
vicious in the name of motherhood:

Time to bait your biggest deep-sea fish-hooks.
Do it while the children are asleep.
Hang them where the Sitka deer foregather,
high enough that wolves will have to leap.

Sunrise. He and I hiked up to check them.
That was when you stared at me. I saw
blood, as if you'd breakfasted on bodies,
smeared like lipstick all along your jaw.

We were savage sisters in the wildwood
bound, like sibling rivals, to collide;
though my skin is furless, I turned she-wolf,
watching coldly as you writhed and died.

Is that shape your spirit, Siren, hurdling
nurse logs in the salal? Are you back?
Lean long-distance runner, are you racing
slow starvation still? Will you attack?

Now I waken, standing in the sea surf
chanting *Sorrow not for Siren*, yet
feeling that I'm hanging from a fishhook,
covered in the carnage of regret.

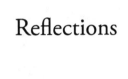

Reflections

Qualicum Sunset

This evening's sunset, though ethereal rose,
is not unique—I've seen its like before
        emblazoning this shore;
others eclipse it, robed and grandiose,
descending suns that, as they disappear,
            draw a train
across the polar ice for half a year—
long, silken night that lets in astral rain.

I see no Ellesmere, but islands smoulder,
anthracite to bank the sunset's fire.
        As twilight's rays retire
the ebb tide bares a sandbar like a shoulder
and ingle benches empty—seabird flocks
            seek nooks of calm;
they search for marsh and carr with goodnight squawks
and sea and sky close like a carmine clam.

In another life I'd clamber Brooks Range talus
or run the Sagavanirktok by canoe,
        my paddle breaking through
a mirrored, mauve aurora borealis.
But this is my life and this fair coast, my home,
            and this setting sun
deserves to be viewed, not with an eye to roam,
but as if it were the first and only one.

Bedtime Story

The sun has smouldered low. Its flaxen light
drizzles through the birches to the snow
where sheep stand still as hay bales, beige on white.
A shepherd with a shoulderful of straw,
brindled by the shadows, softly walks.
The sheep flock round; he swings his load to strew
the strands on pillowed drifts like yellow locks,
then hastens homewards bearing sustenance
against the ghostly dark. He holds small hands
and spins his children tales of happenstance
and golden fleeces in enchanted lands.
Their minds woolgather. Snuggled down in bed,
they drift on snowy pillows; yellow strands
of hair glow like the hay their father spread.

You Hold My Hand

You hold my hand in case I fall
though you are wee and I am tall,
and as you do you stop to show
me where the Dancing Daisies grow
to cheer the Frog-Prince in the wall.

We hear a pheasant cock; his call
enthralls us so we start to crawl
towards him till we see him crow;
      you hold my hand.

And when I'm huddled in a shawl
of fuddy-duddy folderol,
I'll cleave to what today I know:
that we perceive as we bow low
a Bird King greeting One-So-Small.
      You'll hold my hand.

Day of the Anchorite

The shore is shirred and patterned—ribs remain
from night-ebb, scores of nocturnes, every grain
a note. No Bedouin ever caravanned
        a silk as crimson
as sun reflected on this still-wet sand,
    where moon-snail Buddhas glisten
and squads of killdeers dress in one direction
      for matinée inspection.

The great Pacific yawns to greet the dawn
as, blundering from the night, he wanders on.

A heron darts to chopstick passing herring
then fades, a tideline chalk mark, now unstirring
beside the swinging swell. Small showgirls mill
        and leg some vaudeville,
a sandpiper troupe on tour, dancing until
    they blizzard up for travel
without costumery or worldly goods
      to Arctic latitudes.

A twinge. He also seeks a higher state—
uncumbered and alone, he must migrate.

The storms have fenced the beach with jetsam wattle—
huge logs of driftwood that, when spring tides battle
to reach land's castle walls, mass in a moat
        of wood. These monsters

lie still on solid ground as if afloat
      in time. As seedling youngsters
they grew with roots upwind—they'd hold their ground
      when giants had to bend.

He balance-walks their wreckage to the bush,
where sea swell whoosh becomes a leafy hush.

When moved, the foliage drops its cradled moisture,
the cool, baptismal drippings from a cloister
of Nootka roses. These many-splendoured things,
          rain-washed clean,
are nubile without bridal gowns or rings.
      They're more than pink and green—
no Indian paintbrush, no Monet or Rembrandt
      could make their skins more vibrant.

Soaked, he brushes through them to the deep
rainforest as it wakens from its sleep.

Through skylights in the cedars, light rays pass,
a wind that fans cold cinders—ferns and moss—
to flames of lime. And in that architemple
        millennial art,
its massiveness illuminate, grows simple
      as whisperers impart
the teachings of the forest in the trees
      no other tree-seer sees.

Sap rises in his muscles. Lean and feline,
he forges up the valley to the tree line.

A morning sea mist veils the valley floor
and frees the wooded hills to float and soar
in light that doused the stars. When it burns off,
            it leaves the valley bottom
displayed and splayed and bares the features of
            the coast—a half-made totem
being adzed to inlet mouths and headland beaks
            on weather-tough physiques.

Waves bellow below. A wind whines from a ridge—
he lifts his arms and feels his muscles fledge.

Standing on a mountain, cruciform,
he casts himself into the rising storm
and swallow-dives. Pulsing hidden colour,
            the heart inside his chest
propels him through the rain's grey wires of dolour
            and, though the world is vast,
the shore surf shucks a shell of all it harboured
            and sea wind preens a shorebird.

He skims across an orca's dorsal fin
until he's cut its myths into his skin.

The north is thunderhead; the south and west
are cave light underhung below a crest
of rainbow. Breakers on the headlands catch
            the glow—waves flag their manes
and, foaming, whipped by wind, they rear and crash,
            drop heads to snap their reins,
and make a beauty of themselves that's matchless
            and leaves its watchers speechless.

He spears into their fury like a gannet
and plummets through the mantle of the planet.

The sunset brings a calmness, a release,
then, like a death, the darkness comes in peace.
Though light, like blood in water, rich and red,
               and land were altruistic
to so secede, their very colour dead,
      when they were most majestic,
though moonglow lays its carpet on the ocean,
      an offer of devotion. . . .

He's gone. He needs no friends, no moon for mate,
no bed, no home, no God, no grave, no fate.

River of Refuge

Vancouver Island

I Cataracts

When he's away, he leaves a sign
above the door: *Come in but mind
the bear-board welcome mat!* And there,
across the threshold, you will find
a plywood sheet with line on line
of upward-pointing, two-inch nails.
But he is settled in his lair
when I go fishing there in June.
We spend my steelhead afternoon
beside his river, swapping tales.

His shelter is no backwoods tent.
It's made from logging cable strung
between two trees, a roofline beam
on which a trucker's tarp is hung
and stretched drum-tight. The moose-steak scent
escaping from the door attracts
an old boar bear—it seems to dream
of what's inside but simply prowls
and sometimes woofs but never growls.
Its eyes are pearled with cataracts.

II Channels

We sit and chat beside his boat—
two outboards and a welded hull:
"I bushwhacked here. You came by sea?"
"The mouth's just two miles down. I haul
that beast up through the shoals. A goat
would slip and break its legs there now.
Before they logged, it used to be
the rocks were clean. Now all this slime!
A man might call it payback time.
Rock snot!" The words striate his brow.

He shows me his new wading boots
with soles that interchange from felt
to metal cleats. "These do the job.
And look at this! I bet you knelt
to do your laces up." He shoots
a glance at me as if to gauge
my fitness, stoops, then turns a knob.
One hand. It's easy. Wires tighten.
He smiles. I nod. It's time to lighten
the burdens of advancing age.

III Crossings

"I log-scaled in the northern camps
and saw the old-growth giants fall
then guided, learning grizzlies' ways,
and fished. When waiting out a squall
I've seen males chase their cubs. The scamps

run down and splash into the bays,
get caught in heavy tidal bores,
and wash away in fourteen-knot
currents. Later, I would spot
them climbing out on Island shores.

They say there are no grizzlies here
but I know all the hunting boys—
they reckon seven now, at least.
The other day I heard a noise
and found some tracks—there's one quite near.
One found a guard dog on a chain
up north. A fish farm. Had a feast.
The hundred-pound Rottweiler brute
got eaten clean. They had to shoot
the poor old bear." I see his pain.

IV Confluences

He says the steelhead shoals will school,
then springboard off high tide. "They'll take
five hours to reach this place," a lag
the eagle knows. The waters break
to riffles downstream of the pool.
"In half an hour the bird," he states,
"will perch above them on that snag,"
he points. "He'll watch. When fish arrive
he'll drag one out on his first dive."
It happens just as he relates.

He says, "At dusk a cougar comes
and sits, a bound or two away,"

he points again, "on that flat rock.
I talk to it." He doesn't say
what they discuss. The river thrums
above us in the canyon falls.
He's well aware the cat might stalk
and kill him, yet he loves this place
where wildness is a state of grace
and cedars pillar mountain walls.

V Estuary

His final dog passed on last year.
He keeps its ashes in an urn,
one of a matching pair. He says,
"I've made a will. It says to burn
my body, then to leave us here."
He takes me to a nearby cave
where both of them will rest. I praise
his health and vigour—seventy-five;
few teenagers look more alive—
then leave him to his future grave.

When I get home, I think of him
conversing with the cougar there
beside the river he loves most
and, for a moment, feel the care
he has for it: the light grows dim
and, twilit, on his log, his throne,
the cougar fading like a ghost,
he rolls old boulders in his mind
from caves time bade him leave behind
and, stone by stone, grows more alone.

The Changed and the Changeless

. . . that which is ever changeless. . . must not become elder or younger in time . . .
  —Plato's theory of forms, Timaeus, *38b*

The glacier slides over the lip of the corrie,
spreading its hands on the flanks of the ben;
white fingers chisel the vees from the valleys,
filling the fissures and folds of each glen.

It reaches to where the Teanassie Burn plunges
over a waterfall, chills the cascade
into an iron-hard, ivory outcrop
tinctured with traces of turquoise and jade.

      The "House of the Waterfall" stands by the streamside—
      Gaelic's "Teanassie," a manor of stone—
      tall, ivied gables where cypresses nuzzle,
      lulled by the bees' and the cataract's drone.

      Here lies a garden where fences of birch poles
      shrivelled their silverskin barks in the sun;
      here, beside bushes of lush floribunda,
      bird-netted strawberry cuttings would run.

      Here once a mother's voice blended with bird calls,
      love-filled migrations of laughter and care;
      here once a father conducted a rope swing
      higher and higher through octaves of air.

Bergschrunds are ruptured as, melting, the glacier
shrinks from the waterfall, slinks from the land.
Deep down, a figure appears in the ice-dark,
eager to surface from time's running sand.

Sun-heat exposes the glacier's claw marks—
moraines and striations and tails trailed from crags,
drumlins, erratics, a scarified valley,
meltwater flooded. A small body drags.

    Here once adventuresome deeds at the burnside—
    brothers at play by the summer-deep pool,
    catching small trout from the turbulent spangling,
    drinking cooled sunshine from hands cupped and full.

    Here once a trout, which they never could capture
    telltaled itself at the dusk of each day—
    head-and-tail rises of mythic proportions,
    a bard making lore with each line of his lay.

The waterfall spills from a rib of the valley,
its catchment pool thawed now from pewter to chrome;
under the surface a pallid face slides by,
the boy from the glacier unborn in his home.

    The youth on the rope swing flew higher and higher,
    and leapt from his seat to the arms of the breeze,
    froze there an instant, the apogee lifelong,
    then glided the winds to a land overseas.

He left for one summer, for one summer only.
The Fates of the migrants were playing coin-toss:
"Heads" he is staying, and "tails" no returning.
With homecomings thwarted, his hopes turned to dross.

Then one day the mystery trout surges shorewards
and beaches itself by a murder of crows;
its head and its tail and the bone that connects them
are all that they spare of its giant repose.

The hand of the boy edges out of the water,
his fingers slip slowly up splines of the tail;
behind the wrecked gill plate and up through the gullet,
the boy's index finger deciphers the Braille.

He pulls it back into the sepia silence;
its gill rakers waft in the waters of youth.
The Fates of the migrants bow heads at its passing;
no heads and tails now make a coin-toss of truth.

A jet plane recrosses the ageless Atlantic,
an old heron gliding on world-weary wings;
a greybeard returns to his old home, Teanassie,
and slips back in time as his mother's voice sings.

His hair and his skin are all covered in ice-rime,
his eyes and his teeth are all yellow and lost;
he goes to the pool that bejewelled his boyhood;
it's midsummer frozen and powdered with frost.

And there in the black of the ice that confronts him,
the shape of a body affronts his soul's core—
the tender white face of the boy from the garden,
preserved for the future with future no more.

When I Am Old

Hie me to the hill ground,
the high hill ground of Scotland,
to battle bladed wind blasts
my forebears fought before me,
to stagger stammer-footed,
across the ancient highlands,
> across their schists and drifting bones
> across their shifting ruin-stones,
> where, witchily, the grey pine crones
> still call me to my history.

Leave me there to wayfare
the curlew-plainted wild moor,
to smell the sweet bog myrtle
beside the peaty burn;
to stumble crumbling scree slopes
that roll with rutting stag roars,
> and rediscover drove roads
> and moss embossing lost abodes
> where blood-fed drovers rested loads
> bound south and trudging their return.

Let me find a lone shore
where fishermen lie buried
in graves of wave-flung flotsam
with neither name nor past:
to stand there like a Culdee
as mist trails move unhurried

on island hills and holms and voes
where headlands creaked with yells of crows
as birlinns swooned in hell-bent blows
that heaved the shore and cleaved the mast.

Bear me to the black shed
where the blacksmith shod the plough horse
to plod long narrow furrows
that pleat the folding field,
and when my storm approaches,
I'll stand before its raw force
       by furnace flames of bygone ways,
       and anvils ringing down the days
       that forged my soul and bent these bays;
       I'm of this land—it's here I'll yield,
to the stubble and seeds of the past.

Acknowledgements

My grateful acknowledgements go to the editors of the following publications where these poems, some in earlier versions, first appeared:

Able Muse: "Baying at Two Moons," "For the Crofters," "To the Dead of Winter," "Hay," "Lost Overnight in the Woods," "Murmuration," "Wildfire," and "Your Voice"

Ascent Aspirations: "When I Am Old"

Better than Starbucks: "Regeneration"

Eyes on BC: "To the Bluenose," "Daybreak, Tofino," "Green Hall," "A Many-Splendoured Thing?," "My Nokomis," and "Wolves"

Gatherings: "Creekwalker"

Gray's Sporting Journal: "Jock Scott," "Killing a Coho," and "Shadow-Casting"

Hatches: "Close to Coho"

The Hypertexts: "Qualicum Sunset" and "Songs of the Isles"

Maria W. Faust Sonnet Contest: "Year-Leap"

The New Formalist: "Bedtime Story," "Brothers of the Byre," "Caledonian Pines," "The Changed and the Changeless," "The Combustion of Apples," "In Living Colour," "River Woman," "Woman in the Wind," and "Women of the Ages"

Northwords Now: "Leaving Camustianavaig"

Off the Coast: "Steelhead"

String Poet: "Midwinter Music," "Music Maker," and "Request for a Dance"

129

Sudden Thunder Anthology: "Wizardry"

Thomasgray2016.org: "Laying Ghosts to Rest" and "A Sweetness Absent from the Ocean Air"

Worldwide Toast to Robert Burns: "Immortal Memory"

Thanks also to the editors who republished and anthologised several of these poems, and to the organisers of the following competitions, which gave several of the poems recognition and exposure:

"Murmuration" was the winner of the 2012 Able Muse Write Prize for Poetry, "For the Crofters" was a finalist in the same contest, and "Your Voice" was a finalist in the 2011 run of the contest.

"Midwinter Music" won the 2015 String Poet Prize.

"A Sweetness Absent from the Ocean Air" won Goodreads Poem of the Month for December 2017.

"Laying Ghosts to Rest" and "A Sweetness Absent from the Ocean Air" were honourable mentions in 2014 and 2016 respectively for the Stoke Poges's Thomas Gray Centenary's Inspired by the Elegy contest.

"Immortal Memory" won first equal place in a Worldwide Toast to Robert Burns competition to commemorate the 250th anniversary of his birth.

"Year-Leap" was chosen as a "top three" in the 2017 Maria W. Faust Sonnet Contest.

I wrote most of these poems more for the ear than the eye and I am indebted to many contacts and organisers for opportunities to recite several of them from memory at diverse events including concerts of my wife's band, Celtic Chaos (of which I am a poet member), poetry readings, slam sessions, open mikes, *Able Muse*'s *Eratosphere* podcasts, Celtic events, occasions like weddings, and even a business meeting of the British Columbia Federation of Fly Fishers. Thanks also to Laura Cortese for recording "Women of the Ages" as a song on her album, *Acoustic Project*.

The poems are drawn largely from my own experience, but I am indebted to *The Story of Crofting in Scotland* by Douglas Willis, *The Great Bear Rainforest* by Ian McAllister, and *The Last Wild Wolves* by Ian McAllister for background information used in "For the Crofters," "Creekwalker," and "Siren of the Sea Cliffs" respectively.

I am greatly indebted to Alex Pepple, the proprietor of the *Able Muse* website, and to the many poets with whom I collaborated on that site's excellent metrical workshops. Most of what I know of the craft, I learned there.

Finally, I am greatly indebted to my wife, Joyce, and children, Janie, Ewan, Kate, Kirsty, and Emma, for their love, forbearance, and inspiration.

John Beaton's poetry is metrical and has been widely published in media as diverse as *Able Muse* and *Gray's Sporting Journal*. He wrote a monthly poetry page for several years for the magazine *Eyes on BC* and served for four years as moderator of one of the internet's most reputable poetry workshops, *Eratosphere*. He recites his poems from memory as a spoken word performer and a poet member of the band Celtic Chaos. His poetry has won several awards, including the 2015 String Poet Prize and the 2012 Able Muse Write Prize for Poetry. He is a retired actuary who was raised in the Scottish Highlands and lives in Qualicum Beach on Vancouver Island, Canada.

Also from Word Galaxy Press

David Alpaugh, *Spooky Action at a Distance – Double-Title Poems*

Margaret Rockwell Finch, *Crone's Wines – Late Poems*

Emily Grosholz, *The Stars of Earth – New and Selected Poems*

A.G. Harmon, *Some Bore Gifts – Stories*

Elizabyth A. Hiscox, *Reassurance in Negative Space – Poems*

Sydney Lea and James Kochalka,
The Exquisite Triumph of Wormboy – Poems and Illustrations

www.wordgalaxy.com